4 DA STRUGGLE
PRESENTS

In No Sense

TERRANCE WINN

SUMMERSET
BOOKS

IN NO SENSE
Copyright ©2020 by Terrance Winn

All rights reserved. No part of this book may be reproduced, copied, stored or transmitted in any form or by any means – graphic, electronic, or mechanical, including photocopying, recording, or information storage and retrieval systems without the prior written permission of Terrance Winn or Summerset Books except where permitted by law.

Summerset Books a division of HOV, LLC.
www.Summersetbooks.com
summersetbooks@gmail.com

Covenant Connection Publishing

Cover Design Layout: Hope of Vision Designs
Artwork by: @frostedtatts
Editor: Sharissa Marston

Contact the Author, Terrance Winn at:
terrancetwinn74@gmail.com

For further information regarding special discounts on bulk purchases, please contact terrancetwinn74@gmail.com

ISBN Paperback: 978-1-7357761-2-5

10 9 8 7 6 5 4 3 2 1

Printed in the United States of America

Dedication

First and foremost, I must give thanks to Allah. In Christian terminology, thank God for blessing me to live to tell my story.

I would like to dedicate this book to my loved ones who have gone on before me.

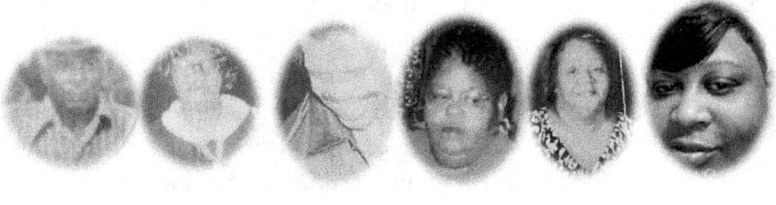

Dedicated to the Best Aunt/Mother In the World (acknowledgments)

My aunt out of thirty years never missed a beat even when my mother became sick and was diagnosed with cancer. My auntie still came with her own personal driver and banker Lecarlos Winn. She never missed a month from sending me money. Her motto is "when I get paid tithes, pastor love offering, Terrance offering everything else falls in place." We hired two lawyers neither one of the lawyers helped. One of the lawyers held onto the money and talked a lot saying "She's so kind hearted." My auntie worked 2 jobs to take care of me and her son Marcellous Dunbar. I would babysit him and clean the house I really thank God for her. Now I'm living with her and her husband which is my Uncle Ozell. She loves me so much and still treats me like I'm 16. She says these things all the time "Terrance where are you going, Terrance hurry back don't be late getting back." I love you always and forever Aunt Lettie.

This is to Aunt Berida

Thank you so much auntie for coming to see me, sending me money and always accepting my phone calls and helping to raise me. I can't express how much love I have for you just know that I will love you forever.

Aunt Joyce Turner/Winn

Even though you are my aunt thru Christ you have been so kind to me. She has been the other driver for the family. I would always hear about how fast you would bring my family members to come see me at 2am I love you a lot for that.

Shelia, Marcellous, Sha and Tawanna

I cannot thank you all enough for sticking with me for 30 years and 7 months. That is a very short time for cousins to stick together for that short amount of time. Marcellous went to the Navy and every chance he got he sent a money order. Now these four are still helping me out so I can make it thru and make the right decisions. I love you all to the moon and back.

To the 6am Tuesday morning prayer group

I ask you all to please keep me in your prayers. Your prayers carried me out so I could be a free man. I'm ever so grateful that you all lifted me up and now I'm home. So a special thank you to Sis A. Terry, Sis R. Dotson, Sis B. Odom, Sis V. Moore, Sis L. Bell.

Dedicated to as my Aunt Lettie says "we have the best pastor in the whole universe" Pastor R. Everett Sr.

I grew up on the Cooper Rd and went to school with the Winn sisters I became their pastor in the year 1992 and they are still friends to this very day. He's just like family he has helped with me a lot by lifting me up in his prayers and continuously praying for me. He was always there for my mom and aunt. Now it is my plan to make you Pastor D. Ray Everett proud of me and I ask that you keep me and my entire family in your prayers.

A special thank you

I want to extend a very special welcome to Rev. Ray Washington. I can remember when I was 10 years old and you would pray for the Winn Family. I love you and may you rest in peace you are gone but never forgotten.

Acknowledgments

One week before the brutal murder of George Floyd, a dear friend, homie, brother of mine by the name of Rufus White was tragically/brutally murdered. He had recently been released from Angola after doing close to two decades. His death hurt because within him there was so much promise. Rest in Heaven homie.

Momma, I feel your presence with each step I take. All the lessons you taught me are with me and will be used. I love you and miss you so much.

Dad (Johnny Lee), you did great by me. From you I learned how to be a man. Because of you, I can accept another man's child as my own. This is the manliest thing anyone can do. I love you.

Sam Dean (dad), I love you forgiving me life. Thank you!

To Lettie, having your love has been so surreal until it's unbelievable. God has blessed me beyond measure through you. No one besides my mother has loved me as you do. It's hard to call you auntie when you have been my mother since my mother died. I will never let you down. I love you. If my life was needed for you to live, I will gladly give my life for you. I love you so much!

To my aunt Birdia, thanks for loving me and supporting me my whole life. The love you have given me is priceless. I will not let you down again.

Shanterria Jones, Shaminique Swan, Ms Rae, Jace, and Ms. Rah Rah, I love you all and I will never voluntarily leave you all again. I can't make up for lost time but I can cherish each day with you all now.

Master Marcus Tyrone Winn, I apologize for not being there for Moon but I'm here now and I won't leave him. You are and will always be my hero. I love you big bro. Walk with me on this journey of positivity.

Moon, please forgive me for leaving you alone in this world. It saddens me to think back on the times you needed your big brother and I wasn't there. Times have changed and I'm here now so know this, I'm with you all the way. Love you.

LeCarlos "CaCa" Winn, I love you cousin. You sacrificed a many of weekends to make sure the family got down that long 4 hour highway to see me. Love is an action and you showed it without having to say it. I love you man and I appreciate you so much. I am always here for you.

Marcellous, man I love you. You've always been more of a brother to me than a cousin. You have placed me in a position to succeed and I won't let you down. I appreciate you!

Roderick, my friend, homie, and now business partner, I love you. We are day 1's.

Curtis Ray Davis, man what do I say – First of all, you're my brotha. I have been down with you since the age of 14. It wasn't positive then but now, it's blossomed into positivity. I love you homie. You have proven your love to me even though you don't show the world this side of you. "Slave State" is a really great book!

Rob & Fox Rich, thank you for loving me. I love you all equally.

Diane, thank you for the love and support. You are a good woman.

Mrs. Terry, you have been by my side throughout this journey and I cannot say "thank you" enough. I appreciate you for everything and I love you.

Joanne, thank you for the years of being by my side as family. I love you!

Anthony Boult, I love you brotha. You have always been with me and every time I needed you most, you were there. In return, I will always have your back and hold you up. I'm here. When will I be able to buy "The Black Embassy" and "The History and Evolution of The Ratchet Movement?"

4 Da Struggle Ent, First lady Brittany, we believe in you so stay humble and always respectful. There are lots of young girls who need positive role models and they need to know that being a rapper doesn't mean being less than a woman.

Poo Cat, stay focused on the bigger picture because we got your back. Let's show another side of The Ratchet and Boss City through intelligence. We need difference, not the regurgitation of sameness. We need awareness of the pitfalls we as black men endure daily. We need leadership. I need you to step up and be this leader lyrically.

To the streets of the Cooper Road or "That Island", thanks for educating me about life and love. We need to regain our pride in ourselves so that others can show us the love we deserve over that fear they display upon learning we're from that Road. Lets return to the moral values of pride and love.

To the whole Ratchet City, let's grow through education because we have fallen behind and no one seems to notice. We have stopped growing in every area growth should be and we aren't prospering. Let's give people a reason to come to our city instead of being overlooked.

D. Brooks, love you homie. Let's do this.

Deezie Caine, I believe in you as being one of the best rapper the world hasn't heard yet. Let's go so that they will.

Ant Bankz, man you are just like Deezie - great - but I need you to want to be great so that we can show the world.

Big Sacc, let's go.

Markey Cannon, come and carry us to paradise.

Viscous The Goddess, you humble me because you are a sister of intelligence and a boss. Oh yeah and you're from that Island. Thank you. I am with you whenever you need me.

Ceno, come on homie. We need you to stay on the grind. Like O, you give me the grooves to sit down and focus. Your tracks are perfect.

Shug, I rock with you homie.

Frankie Tilman, thank you for being a part of this. You are what the world will love and I will give you to them. Just stay 4 Da Struggle because your voice is definitely 4 Da Struggle.

Cuznjed, love you homie.

Poppa Locc, love you as well. Let's Free My People until I see my people.

Ronald "DC" Reynolds, you are my brother and I love you. Andre, you're my brother. I love you.

GG, you're my brother. I love you.

To the local talent, keep striving.

To my Angola family, Monie my best friend (along with Quinton) since kindergarten, I love you and will do whatever it takes to get you home. Boo, BJ, D. Mims, Playa Ray, Jr Boy, GY, Poat, Trill, PJ, Poppa, Fred Taylor, both Lil E's, Gator, Charlie Brown, Derrick Price, Joe Franklin, The Islamic Community, Sadiq, Sami, Blackman, White Mike, the one and only Moneyhall, Gage, Marlo Mike, Lib, TG, Boobie Earl, Troy 4ever Young, 2five, Prince, Lil Randy, Dre Anderson, Pop the boss, Keith Morse, Tim Bo, Six O, Wacco, Cedar Grove Boo (my big brother for real), there are so many, too many, to name but you all know I got plenty more books so I will name you guys...Can't forget Hooks one of the best inmate lawyers in the world.

RIP to all those I love. MoMA, I will make you proud. I miss you so much and you see my tears when I awake needing you or when Moon and I talk. I'm so sorry for not listening. I miss you so much until it becomes almost unbearable at times, but Moon keeps me focused. I will make you proud!

Marcus, I miss you big brother. I love you. Watch over us.

Aunt Pudding, I love you and miss you so much. I carry the lessons you taught me.

Uncle Andy, I love and miss you.

Timoko, I still call your name because I am in disbelief. I love you sis. Miss you so much.

Uncle Andrew, miss you and love you.

Granddad Jimmy Winn, Grandma Clotile Winn, I miss you all so much and love you. To the Winn and Miles family, I really love you all.

Gary Louis, Carey, Steve, Roderick Maple, Roderick Harris, Half Pint, DC, Alvin Moore Jr, Ernest Knighton, C Bo, Irvin Winn, Iron Mike D, Quincie Foster (We Bang bcuz of you so I won't let them forget).

To Shirley Bullard and all the members of Ruth Circle at Lake Bethlehem Baptist Church, thank you for all your prayers and support.

To those I forgot, please forgive me this is only the beginning.

Contents

Introduction.................................... 13
Chapter 1... 17
Chapter 2... 21
Chapter 3... 25
Chapter 4... 29
Chapter 5... 33
Chapter 6... 37
Chapter 7... 41
Chapter 8... 45
Chapter 9... 49
Chapter 10 59
Chapter 11...................................... 65
Chapter 12 69
Chapter 13 73
Chapter 14 77
Chapter 15 85
Chapter 16 91

Introduction

From a teenager to an adult in the blink of an eye. That was my destiny. At the age of sixteen, I committed a heinous crime which altered my life as I had known it. Now I belonged to the Louisiana Criminal Justice System, a permanent resident of the Louisiana State Penitentiary (better known as Angola). My crime, murder. In an attempt to murder one human being, I unfortunately murdered an innocent man. Handed down the maximum sentence of life in prison, my life had virtually ended with the precious life that I had taken. Because of my anger, I single-handedly destroyed my family and the family of my victims. Acting without thinking is the worse thing anyone can do. It lacks the most basic fundamental of humanity, compassion.

Many of us, or should I say all of us, at some point in our lives, have dealt with anger issues. Some are even controlled by it. When our anger escalates, it's best to seek support from those who can help you manage it. This is even true when attempting to manage finances. Anger management is the key to who goes to prison, to the graveyard or be successful. Management of our anger can allow us to explore a whole new world. Our eyes are opened wider for us to see things differently, respond differently, and engage differently.

Most people who are in the system attribute their situation to poverty. Prisons are filled with people who live way below the poverty line. This also contributes to anger. Think about it, who wants to see their mother struggling to care for her family. Not knowing where your next meal is coming from creates a different type of anger. Poverty has its own language, traits, culture, cry. People who are poorer tend to react to life differently than those who well-to-do. This is also true of person who comes from a two-parent household versus a one-parent household.

Life experiences, whether it touches us directly or indirectly, create emotions that cause us to react in ways that could be detrimental. Often times, we see it as being who we are, or that it is what it is. In order to begin the healing process, we must dig deeper into ourselves to actually see how we came out this way. Before traveling down the road to destruction, we must at least try to fix our own problems. Bad boys/girls look good on TV but in reality they end up dead or in prison. The criminal system is waiting in the background for those who are "bad."

In no sense should innocence be destroyed by adopting the ways of our environment. Sure we love our neighborhoods, gangs. We even represent them, throwing up our hoods. What is the positive in it? Falling prey to the influences of negativity will lead to a life of detriment. For example, if you hang around negative people who involve themselves in negative things, you will eventually do what they do or be guilty by association.

In No Sense of living should we allow negative influences to control our lives to where the outcome will be negative. We use negative/disrespectful terms in anger towards one another and in a lot of cases the outcome is bad. Certain words or phrases trigger our anger and causes us to lose control. Music has the distinction of bad influence. Far too many people trapped in the system will tell you they were listening to a type of music which compelled them to commit a crime. The realness of music exposes the untold truths of living in poverty, living in fear, living hard lives. Frustration evolves from the fact that there is little that can be done about this life that you are living at the moment and you just react.

In No Sense should we not have compassion for others because there will come a time when we all will cry out for compassion.

In No Sense should we not have empathy for others. Empathy makes us take a step back and think about ourselves in someone else's shoes. How would we feel if we were the ones being hurt because of the anger of another. How would we feel if we were the ones being robbed. Placing yourself in another person's shoes is the only way to show empathy, to rationalize and have compassion for our fellow human being.

In No Sense do I want anyone to walk in my shoes. I want better for you.

I grew up listening to music of the gospel, trying to emulate the Apostle Paul. My environment was hostile. On top of that, I experienced a major life change at a young age. My older brother, who I love dearly, died. All of my compassion, my empathy, my hospitality died along with him. My life changed drastically. My family became ashamed of the things I started to do but in order to survive in the streets, I had to "bring the pain. The pain I brought came in the form of me joining the Crips gang and so I started to bang. Church, spiritual singing, all of those things stopped for me. There was no longer beauty in the world. My focus was only on doing the will of Satan; terrorizing my own community, defying rhetorical cries of unity, retaliating for my home boys' eulogies (oddly). My character was being defined through my adversity. Disturbingly, "bad boys" were more accepted commercially. I strayed farther from the paths of prophets in search of profit. Hate had consumed me and I willing disobeyed. There was no repenting for me because of the resentment that had filled my life. Opinions and judgments didn't matter to me. I stopped caring for stopped caring about people's judgment.

The autobiography of Malcolm X made the positive change on my life that I had been longing for. After reading it, my misanthropic optic was sucked up by an invisible vacuum. It was Allah who became captain of my life. Now, positivity holds me captive. I have been captured…

Chapter 1

Born happy and healthy on October 19, 1973, I brought a radiant smile to the face of Dorothy Winn, my mother. Several days later, I arrived home to the Cooper Road, the neighborhood I grew up in. My street, Willie Mays, was one of many named after famous black people who were greatly recognized in the Cooper Road community. My mom and I shared a room in my grandparents' home. Also living with my grandparents was my Aunt Birdia, who had just gave birth to her daughter, Timoko, the June before I was born. I entered my home for the first time carried in the arms of my uncle, Andrew, who had come all the way from Los Angeles to visit. My older brother, Marcus, would also share a room with my mom and I. The first time I recall meeting the person who had impregnated my mom was around the time I was four or five years old. I vaguely remember him ever coming around. One vivid memory I do have of him is when I was about three years old. He had sliced my mother beneath her jaw. It wasn't funny at the time but all my aunts and my grandparents beat him unconscious and threw him off the porch. It's funny how children are able to recollect experiences from younger ages.

My brother, Marcus, was my best friend. Marcus never walked or talked. He could do nothing on his own. I loved him, and to this day still love him, with everything that I have in me. I made it my mission to protect him from all hurt and danger.

Tawanna, another one of my cousins, was the child of Lillie Pearl, my mom's oldest sister. My cousin, Timoko, and I were raised together and we were taught to protect each other as sisters and brothers would. The difference between us and Tawanna was that Tawanna was being raised by both of her parents.

My family was large and close-knit. We often displayed our love for each other. I looked up to my cousins, Andrew, and Tony. They lived in Los Angeles so I didn't see them much. But in Shreveport, there were many that I looked up to. Bay (Aunt Lillie's son), Wolf and Carey (cousin Mickey's sons), Mike and Pig (cousin Betty's sons) and Alvin Jr, Gary and Ron (cousin Alvin's sons) all looked after me growing up. These guys taught me how to fight, how to act and how to treat girls. Wolf was the real lady's man. I thought I was more like him because we both were left-handed. My mother and Bay Bay's mother were sisters. He was my favorite. When Bay was around, I knew I was protected. He shielded me like I was his little brother and he could throw down if he had to.

As our family was close-knit, we all lived on the same street. Across from my house was Aunt Lillie and her four kids, Shannon, Jimmy, Bay Bay and Tawanna. Two houses over were Aunt Lettie and her daughter, Shelia (her son, Marcellous, wasn't born yet). Between them was cousin Betty. My stepfather, his brother, sisters, and parents all lived on the same side of the street as I did.

In our neighborhood, there was a game room where you would go to hang out. It was located down the street from

CHAPTER 1

where my family lived. Across the street from the game room was a trail that led to the roughest projects in our hood, Peach Street Projects. These projects were filled with poor black people who basically had nowhere else to go. In these projects, you could always count on someone being murdered, stabbed, shot or a fight going on. Life there was extremely rough and it reflected poverty. Most people who lived there were tough, either by nature or by circumstance. One day, my cousins and I were at the game room. I was maybe ten or eleven. Three guys from the projects walked in. Immediately, my guard was turned on just as everyone who encountered someone from the projects. I was standing beside the Galaxy game with a quarter already in the machine awaiting my turn to play. The three guys acknowledged my cousin. The youngest of the crew walked over by me and said that he had the next game. I responded by saying "no, you don't" because my quarter was in the machine before he got there. I admit I was a little scared because he was bigger than I was and he was from the projects. Even though I was a young boy, I was known in the street for being tough and being a good fighter. Even kids from my elementary school (Pine Grove) were putting my name out there for being tough. I was not aware that this guy already knew who I was and that he was trying to test me to see if he could pull my cord (as in hoe cord). He threatened to beat me up because I stood up to him. I played the game and tried my best to stall so he wouldn't beat me up outside. My cousin, Bay, peeped me out and told me it was time to go. I let him know what was up and that I did not want to get jumped by whoever was waiting for me outside. He laughed and said that he would handle his end but he wanted me to just walk out and punch Cat Gut (the guy's name) hard and to keep punching him. We walked out of the game room and a group of guys from the projects were waiting on us. I hid my fear, walked straight up to Cat Gut, and punched him in the face as hard as I could. I surprised everyone. Then I punched him again before he hit me back hard. We fought a little. I looked over and saw my cousin being jumped. My fear set back in and I took off running.

My standing up to Cat Gut got me way more recognition than I hoped for and even some respect from the projects. The people from the projects thought people who lived in houses were weak. It was hard to gain respect if you did not live in the projects. Growing up, I was not allowed to go to the projects. It was off-limits to me. My family feared the danger and did not want me hurt. I listened to them for a while until I reached middle school (Linear Junior High). There my life would take another turn. There was where I met Donnell "White Boy" Rogers. White Boy, who had a twin sister, wasn't white but he was very light-skinned. He had respect in the projects. He took me there for the first time. He didn't let anybody bother me but I still had to fight. It was their form of initiation to the projects. After my fight was over, there were others who wanted to fight me. White Boy said "no" and that was the end of that. Even though I gained respect from those guys, my cousin was still very upset at me for running away. He handled his business and wanted me to stand my ground.

Chapter 2

My family saw promise in me and therefore, they stood behind me and supported me in my endeavors. I was smart, athletic, and was a leader; all traits they believed would lead me out of the hole of the Cooper Road. Success was the road map they tried to lay out for me. Going to church was big in my family. I sang in the church choir and at an early age, I even wanted to be a preacher. As my friendship grew with White Boy and the more I hung out in the projects, that aspiration just faded away. Things changed again for me when I became friends with George "GG" Lewis. We met while we both were trying out for the basketball team. Initially we were adversaries because we played the same position. GG was a good player with a learned shot while I had raw talent. He came from a two-parent household. He lived on the other side of the neighborhood, from the Russell Road side. His side of the hood did not get along with our side of the hood. GG, and most guys from his side of the hood, were different. They all had dads at home.

GG came from a well-to-do family. His father's guidance was evident in everything he did, especially decision making. He wasn't a coward, yet during those formative years only the most rugged got respect. GG became my best friend. He once introduced me to his relative, Robert Parish, who was a NBA legend. I had established myself as rugged. If anyone messed with GG, they were essentially messing with me and that was a problem. I took this stance with most of my childhood friends who were viewed as soft due to having good families.

Several things happened that changed the course of my life. The first was my cousin, Alvin Moore Jr, innocently being killed by the State of Louisiana. This gave me my very first taste of the unfairness in the justice system. I can remember my mom and aunts crying and talking about his case although I didn't fully understand. Alvin Jr was the oldest of his brothers, Marvin, Gary, Ron, and Kevin. I was older than Kevin by two years. Marvin was in the military at the time. I was a child and wanted to know what was happening with Alvin Jr. Marvin came home on leave from the military with his uniform still on. I asked Marvin, "Why don't you get the president to let Alvin Jr come home?" Tears came out of his eyes and he ran in his parents' home. I asked my cousins, Mike and Pig, what I did wrong and they said "nothing" but tears were in their eyes also. I didn't understand the magnitude of things. In no sense did I understand that innocence was the hardest thing to prove in the court of law.

On the night the state murdered Alvin Jr in Angola prison, my mom and aunts were there picketing. I was home with my cousins, Timoko, Tawanna, Sheila, Shannon, and my baby brother, Jarvis. We were awaiting word to come down from the then governor, Edwin Edwards, as new evidence had been presented proving Alvin Jr.'s innocence. We saw our mothers on the news outside the prison gate with their picket signs. I fell asleep while waiting. Awakened by Sheila's loud crying, I asked my cousin Shannon what had happened. She told me

CHAPTER 2

that they killed Alvin Jr knowing he didn't do anything wrong. Next thing that happened; I was asleep and my Aunt Birdia woke me up crying telling me my cousin, Wolf, had been killed by his best friend. I screamed and cried in disbelief. It hurt me so bad that I tried to take my skin off. I had to go with her to pick my mom up from work. As I was lying in the back seat crying, New Edition's song, *Is This The End*, was playing on the radio. I started to cry louder as I was in so much pain.

I remember the effect Wolf's death had on so many people. For days, cousin Betty's yard was filled with people. Murk (who was considered family but was really a close family friend who grew up down the street from us) tried to explain to me what happened. He was there when Wolf was killed. Ironically, all of my cousin's childhood friends and his brother, Lil Wolf (Carey) were there the night he was killed. At this time, our neighborhood had produced a gang that garnered nationwide attention, the 22 gang. This gang's territory was the Russell Road and was where my cousin was killed. I didn't understand how his friend could kill him when we were taught not to harm our friends. I thought the friend had defected to the 22 gang and killed him but this wasn't the case.

At Wolf's funeral, I sat by my cousin, Duke. Duke was also there the night of the fight which led to Wolf's death. I watched how packed the funeral was. There were so many people there until many had to stand outside and wait to view the body. I remember watching ladies faint, some tried to take Wolf out of the casket, one even tried to get in the casket with him. Then I saw all of the 22 gang members come through to pay their respects. I kept questioning Duke. I then told him I was going to be like Wolf. It was at that moment I watched everyone grieve his loss that I realized how much power he had.

A few weeks later, I went to the skating rink with Bay Bay, Murk, Larry, Duke, Keith, Steve (Murk's brother) and Lil Wolf. The skating rink was located on Martin Luther King Drive (which ran all the way through our hood), but it was on the Russell Road end. Everything went well inside the skating rink. The skating rink was the place to be on Friday and Saturday nights. There would always be some kind of trouble afterwards due to the 22 gang. They were a force to be reckoned with and they were always at odds with our end. Well that particular night, Steve got into an altercation with a member of the 22 gang. Murk tried to break it up and he ended up getting stabbed.

Chapter 3

A learning point in my life came when my best friend and older brother died. I was the starting corner back on a 1-loss team that was about to play for the state championship in New Orleans. I was an honor roll student. When my brother died, all my motivation died with him. I quit the team and stayed in the house. All of my life I questioned God about my brother's condition. I wanted my brother to be normal like everyone else so we could do things together like brothers did. I was always getting into fights. Sometimes I would come home, go into the room he shared with my grandmother and cry while talking to him. I wanted protection from my older brothers. I had to fight older brothers all the time because I beat up the brothers my age. I just wanted my brother to walk with me and he couldn't do anything due to his condition. To me, God had cursed me because I didn't have a father and my older brother was handicapped. At school, I always fought the guys who made fun of the handicapped because my brother had a handicap. In my own way, I protected him from all the ridicule. Only childhood friends from our section knew about him. Very few people were even allowed to visit with him.

My brother died at age 16. I was 13 and Moon (our baby

brother) was 7. A few months after my brother passed, my mother took sick and would never return wholly to herself.

It was then that I learned that my cousin, Wolf, died as the result of a fight over a dice game. People from our side of the hood joined in the dice game with the 22 gang. One thing led to another and they started fighting. Lil Wolf punched Birdette and Birdette started fighting him, which led to Wolf defending his brother and getting stabbed to death.

Exactly one block away, Murk got stabbed behind a fight. Alvin Jr lost his life because he was having sex with a married white woman. Her husband murdered her but before she died her last word to the cops was "Aaron." Her husband's name was Aaron. They arrested Alvin Jr and let Aaron remain free, although Aaron confessed afterwards.

There were so many bad things going on in my life until it didn't take much persuasion to get me to try marijuana. One day at Green Oaks High school, me, Lil Willie, his cousin Jerome, and JeCarlos (Champ), were caught smoking weed. Only Champ and I received a citation and ultimately probation.

From marijuana I graduated to alcohol with this same collection of friends. Alcohol seemingly gave me the ingredients to cope. Everyone around me was drinking. I enjoyed drinking away my pain, enjoyed partying tipsy or going to concerts drunk. To me, alcohol made me function better.

The first time I got kicked out of school was for drinking alongside Champ, Monie (my friend since kindergarten), Rodrick Emory, and Jamaal. I could see the hurt and disappointment in my mom's eyes when she picked me up from school. The whipping I got didn't compare to the pain I caused her. Although I kept doing dumb stuff, I was a momma's boy and my mother loved me with everything she had.

CHAPTER 3

As had become the thing, every parent blamed me even though I was the youngest. It was always "I betcha that Winn boy had y'all out drinking and skipping school." Mothers of my friends had an image of me as being the baddest kid and that image circulated from mother to mother. This brought shame to my mother and aunts due to our family having a good reputation in our neighborhood. Yet here I was doing all types of crazy stuff while influencing friends to do crazy stuff too. When everything boiled down, I was viewed as the ringleader because I was a natural leader.

My desire to be a preacher ended when Alvin Jr. was murdered because it didn't seem right that all my family's prayers went unanswered. I didn't do any drastic blaspheming. I simply stopped praying and going to church even though my family pushed me to attend. I preferred hanging with friends or sneaking over to see girls.

I was all over the neighborhood and my friends varied because I could blend into any crowd comfortably. There were the guys I hung with at school. These guys went to school regularly, excelled academically, weren't into the streets, but they loved to party and have fun. Then there were my athletic friends and my core friends which were those on the other side of school. I balanced them out by keeping each group separate because the street friends didn't mesh well with my friends from school. although they knew each other.

One night our girls' basketball team was playing one of our archenemies in school as well as neighborhood. At this time, my name was well-known throughout the city. When we arrived, the guys from Lakeside, Allendale, and the Bottom (the primary hoods that attended Booker T Washington High School) were calling my name at the game. Alongside me were Champ and our homie, BK, who had left the hood as a baby and grew up in Los Angeles. My daughter's mom played for our girls' basketball team so my arrival and the murmur that went along with it reached her as a Bottom Boy was talking to her. She quickly ended the conversation just as some of our schoolboys came running to me because the Bottom Boyz were trying to make them leave. I walked out with my two-man crew and confronted them, letting them know there would be problems if anything happened to anyone of my schoolboys. There were no more words spoken because they knew I meant business; this isn't to say they were cowards; it's just stating facts on what happened that particular night.

Chapter 4

In No Sense should Innocence be destroyed by the evils of the environment. Shreveport has always been a city of gangs so when the Crips and Bloods culture came, it was highly embraced. The gang culture was brought to Shreveport by those who originally lived in Shreveport but had moved to Los Angeles. They returned with drugs/crack cocaine. Initially, the drugs changed the city but then the media started placing tags on certain hoods, affiliating them with the gangs. This attention really made L.A. gangs take off in Shreveport.

On the Island, better known as the Cooper Road, Champ and I played a pivotal role in implementing Crips on our side of the hood. We were the first duo to claim the gang which ultimately chained us to change. We were young and impressionable so we couldn't see the destruction we would cause by accepting the culture of L.A. Crack cocaine came through us and like Pac said, "it was strange how it rocked us." The evidence of the destruction we ushered in became visible through the carnage of respectable families. This small drug literally rocked our community off its very principled core.

The impact of our accepting this lifestyle and helping to spread it through our influence on friends couldn't be determined by a 13-year-old (me) and a 14-year-old (Champ). This is the same limited prism of most people who commit crimes. We never think about the impact we caused. We never see the pain, anguish, and the turmoil of the loved ones nor of the victims because all we see is our anger or need. This is wrong on every front unless it's a case of your defending yourself. Crime impacts humans in a wide variety of ways and it's not one-sided, our actions impact our families also.

Champ was a true hustla. This was his imprint. He had come up in the projects well-liked and one of the best dancers in the hood. When his family moved out of the projects, he moved next to my stepdad which was down the street from me. There was only one homie who could out hustle Champ and he hadn't come home from prison yet. His name was G. But as a youngsta, Champ knew how to make money. Me, I was a combination of hustla and enforcer. Champ and I shared hustling duties but I did a lot more in the street; thus the recognition when we went places.

Through our gang affiliation, we started doing a lot of stuff outside of the hood. One night Champ, Shitty, E, myself and Anthony (son of the sheriff who had busted Champ, Lil Willie, Jerome, and I smoking weed) went to a block party downtown bordering on the Bottom. This was the Bottom Boyz' territory but we came to party, not to beef. We had already been drinking and smoking on our way to the party. Once we arrived, I told everyone not to split up for nothing and that if a situation jumped off that didn't involve us, we weren't paying it any attention. Again this was Bottom Boyz' territory so they would be out in large numbers looking to hustle any way they could. We got out the car and started walking along the jam packed streets. The Bottom Boyz set up a hustle through a fight. Anthony, lame to the game, got separated from us and became

CHAPTER 4

Bottom Boy prey. He was wearing a real Louis Vuitton cap, pouch, and jewelry. One of them hit him while two others took the Louis and the jewelry. A female saw us and pointed. Without thinking, I went behind one of the Bottom Boyz and chased him into the Bottom under one of the high sitting shotgun houses. It was a very dangerous move but I wasn't scared. The police then swarmed us and I had to run.

Several days later, I caught three assault charges stemming from an incident that happened in junior high and it landed me in juvey hall for the second time. When I arrived, the second day, room rec was ending so I wasn't able to check out who else was in there. I went to my room and listened to the talk while trying to fight off the claustrophobia. From all of the talk, you would've thought guys were enjoying themselves. I just took it all in with my eyes closed. I hated being there with no control over anything. I hated hurting my mom and aunts because they loved me when no one else did. My life had gone off track. I no longer gave off the hope of my one day making it out of the hood through sports. I no longer gave off the assurance that I would attend college and succeed. An old timer, ex con by the name of Cadillac Black, once told me, "Boy you're going to the penitentiary for murder" but I never took heed to his words. I thought they were just words. Plus my environment celebrated murderers so it didn't bother me. I was 14 when he said it. Now here I sat on a concrete slab for a bed, directly across from a toilet/sink combo and I fought back tears because I didn't want to be there. Yet I knew I had to be tough or it would look bad on my hood or my set. "I'm Terrance Winn" is how I thought, totally egotistical.

When the doors opened for rec again, I walked out, entered the room, and got me a seat. A stranger walked up saying the seat was his. Before I could respond a dark skinned guy, real stocky built asked me my name, so I told him. He, in turn, said that I was from the Cooper Road and about my business. The guy moved on but a crowd gathered around. Another guy stood beside the stocky guy and asked me if I attended the block party. I said, "yes." He said he was the one that I chased beneath the house. So, in a loud voice he sealed me. "This is Terrance Winn and I know he's about his business because can't no one run through the Bottom and live to tell about it. Man, I'm Moon Head and this is Black."

As he spoke, I saw two more guys I went to school with from the Cooper Road, Shay Shay and Lavelle. We were beefing so I knew there wouldn't be an alliance, but I also knew I could carry my weight in there without help.

Chapter 5

No matter how much I hurt my mom and my family, they never let me down. This was a fact I always had. My mom never missed a visit when the judge refused to let me go home. She loved me so much until she was even concerned about what I was eating while locked up. During one of her earlier visits to see me, she asked me if she could bring me something to eat. I didn't know the answer. We asked the guard and he said she could, only if she fed everyone, including the girls. So she told me to ask everyone what they wanted eat. The majority said they wanted pizza. The next night, to everyone's disbelief, we all ate pizza. The next night, it was chicken and we continued eating like that until I was released.

Practically everyone there had already been sentenced or expected to be. Either they were going down south to Scotland (Baton Rouge) or to Monroe. Moon Head had received three years and expected me to follow suit but I told him my mother wasn't going to let me go down south. Later that evening, I was told that I would be transferred to the Rutherford House. At the time, I didn't know what it was but everyone else did. Moon Head and Black gave me hugs and Moon Head told me, "Man, you got a good momma, that woman love you."

The Rutherford House is located in Highland, a once upper middle class subdivision, where almost every house had appeal. It consisted of four big houses (three for boys, one for girls). The house I was assigned to sat next door to the girls, two blocks away from the school we attended. The set-up was unique to me.

Upon entering the house, it never occurred to me that I didn't have to be there. I focused on getting out and avoiding going down south. I never had worries about being able to handle myself because I could and I knew that I would receive "Big Dawg" status as I had in juvey being who I was from the street. My way of thinking matched that of my environment and it was toxic because it didn't seem odd or in need of change. Violence had been all I knew, both via direct involvement or from what I saw daily. Problems didn't get resolved verbally, no one walked away to live to see another day. Everyone faced things head on and most endings were tragic. It's what my environment taught me. In theory, my environment prepared me to take a fall, represent the hood, and come back the same way I went in. Very little prepared me to think differently outside of my home environment. The streets were all structured the same; get it how you live or live by the sword and die by it - but never cry. This was a universal language in the streets. It was passed down and I accepted it as I did so many other things that went against what my family taught me or the positives passed on to me by friends' parents, who saw me going astray. Friends like GG's father, my then pregnant girl, Lisa's father, Monie's father, White Boy's father, my cousin who happened to be a lawyer, Carl Servyn, Eddie Marshall's father, Rodrick and Murk's father, my step (I'm ending this prefix because he accepted me as his own and he is my two brothers' father),

CHAPTER 5

two of my junior high principles and numerous teachers and coaches all tried to keep me on the right path when they saw me going off course.

I made promises but I also made a bad decision to follow the codes and conduct of the streets. My choices weren't limited. I simply chose wrong. All those telling me about being on the road to prison, I categorized them as trying to jinx me (the term "hating" hadn't been established then). It never occurred to me that they were telling me something good because they had lived long enough to have seen bad things happened to guys with promise, who were now making poor choices. My youth wouldn't let me see this and it cost me dearly.

When I arrived at the Rutherford House, they were getting ready to go eat dinner which meant everyone had to get in a van and travel the block to the school's cafeteria. As everyone was coming out of their rooms, Pops, the man in charge, called group (which I would later learn meant everyone report to the living room within minutes for a discussion). I sat alone on a chair as ten guys quickly appeared and took their seats. Of all the guys, there was only one person I knew and we were archenemies. His name was Lil Jay and he was responsible for bringing the Bloods gang to the Queensborough neighborhood. We had had our share of run-ins so I felt we wouldn't survive together in this house.

I was introduced to everyone as they were to me and then we all got in the van and went to the cafeteria. It was a Friday night. This stood out because I learned that we could gain weekend furloughs for good behavior. Also, where I was housed, we were allowed to eat with the girls on special weekends.

Being the new guy earned me some attention, especially from the girls. I wasn't really thinking about girls at the time because

I was focused on Lil Jay.

After we ate and got back to the house, Lil Jay asked me if he could have a word with me. We stepped away from everyone to have a conversation. He wanted me to know that he would be going home really soon and that he did not want any beefing between him and I. He did not want anything to interfere with him getting released on time. We came to an agreement that we would not beef while there.

Lil Jay was only seventeen years old but street smart beyond his years. We were doing something unheard of; placing our differences aside for the greater good and the streets respected it.

During this time, my oldest daughter, Shanterria, was only a baby and "Self-Destruction", an East Coast collaborative rap song by most of their heavyweights, was the big song at the time.

Chapter 6

The structure of the Rutherford House was designed to make you a better functioning human being. They equipped you with all the tools to succeed to not be a recidivist. The staff was very caring and supportive. With this being said, Lil Jay had everyone eating from his hands. He was their star and without any doubt, he was the leader, not just in the house we were assigned to, but the entire Rutherford House. He had a powerful personality plus he was charming. Every staff member had high expectations of him to return to society and succeed.

A few days after my arrival, there was a basketball game between Rutherford House and Cool Springs. I was asked by the coach to participate. The team had been established for a while so I didn't start in the game. They didn't know if I was a good player. As the game got going, I could see that our best player was big and that Cool Springs' guard outmatched ours. Coach let them play for a while before pulling our guard out and sending in another. Same results, the guard on the other team was shining. Finally, the coach called me and gave me a few pointers. I went to the score table and entered the game. It didn't take long for me to show my skills and outplay the guard on the opposing team. Our big center and I won the game for our team but he and I clashed slightly. This showed my attitude of not being one to mess with.

Because of the basketball game, I received the attention of the staff. My natural leadership qualities started to show. It wasn't long before I was getting the Lil Jay comparisons. Lil Jay and I had become friends and we started to understand each other.

Again the structure was designed for you to succeed. Violence was almost nonexistent at Rutherford House because of all the luxurious benefits offered. For example, if you hadn't started to receive weekend furloughs, there was movie night, shopping trips (for those who had saved money from weekly allowance), pool outings and other fun things that were offered just to show another side of life.

Then there was the structure of always having a witness. It was designed like that. No one could talk to anyone from another house without having someone with you. From a street perspective, that seemed invasive, yet if you can examine it closer it saved a lot of us from going to prison because an alibi was always good.

And then there was the calling of group. Now that was really frowned upon from a street perspective because it entailed ratting unless used for the right reason. Group was called and designed to problem-solve constructively. Let's say someone stole my jeans from my room. My street mentality says to harm a thief because in the real world nobody likes thieves. Alright, I'm a product of my environment so I learn who stole my jeans. I wait until he's at his most vulnerable and I attack him unmercifully. The outcome; he's messed up while I return to juvenile hall with a new charge that will either land me in the parish jail or on the road down south. But if I take the lessons learned in the group, listen to the advice of peers, accept the apology of the perpetrator, and move on with my jeans, I'm winning. A simple way of thinking for a change - for the better.

Another thing that was good about the functioning of group was this; it was a support group, something we all needed to stay on the right path. In some environments, there's a breeding pool of negativity, meaning problems are solved with violence and this violence is accepted as normal. It's so normal until it becomes expected in most situations. Within these environments, it's hard to walk away from something due to how people are taught to perceive you. Respect is everything in these environments. This is why people within these environments reflect violently to set examples for everyone to know not to try anything against you or the consequences will be harsh. We don't want the label of being "soft" or "weak" because it leads to problems down the road. However, we don't' recognize this fact. The overwhelmingly majority of our peers aren't violent and they respond to the same situations we face with diplomacy and everything works out fine. Real life example; my friends and I were at the NWA concert and a guy was getting initiated into the Bloods gang. His target was - us. He snuck (hit someone who is unaware) White Boy and we all started fighting. A few weeks later, we saw this same guy at the skating rink. White Boy is encouraged to smash him and it's sinking in. White Boy walked off and started pacing. I walked over to him and asked him what was wrong. He looked at me with tears in his eyes and said "If I kill him, my dad is going to kill me. Cuz I don't want to be locked up the rest of my life for nothing." I looked at him strangely because this was foreign to me. So I said, "Whatever you decide, I'm with you but I really want to do something to that dude. It's your decision though." No, I wasn't trying to diffuse the situation but I was being a friend. Now, staying with the example: I was snuck inside of a different concert, LL Cool J, and when I saw the guy weeks later, my homies led the attack. No one tried to deescalate the situation. Same circumstances, different outcome due to different support groups.

Positives in life are always better than negatives. Sure in the moment, the negative feels so good. Yet the outcome of negative is a life of looking back on your mistakes thinking, "If I had only chosen the other route." If we look at all the people living the right way, we will see that they are living good free lives. Nothing is better than being free and thinking correctly trying to help someone over hurting them.

Chapter 7

In order to want better, you must do better.

Before coming to the Rutherford House, Lil Jay had a drug problem while I had a drinking problem. At the Rutherford House, the structure was for us to succeed as I can honestly print out 31 years later. (I couldn't see that at the time and I hardly gave it thought while trying to figure out how to do a life sentence). Anyone with alcohol or drug problems was asked to attend meetings. I started attending A.A. meetings with a staff member, who was a recovering alcoholic. Being young, I thought this was lame plus I felt as though I had my drinking under control. I felt it lame to admit my problems to strangers, open my life to strangers, because in my environment, this wasn't done but I attended half-heartedly.

False courage and strength are reasons why I drank alcohol. I lied to myself like being drunk made me have more fun when this was only a lie. How can you have a good time when you're not in complete control of your body functions and your memory is impaired. Whatever problems we're trying to erase through drinking will be your same problems sober. Nothing takes away the problem but working on it. We have fun when we're sober, remembering every moment.

My baby girl, Shaminique, entered the world while I was on

my eight-hour furlough.

A.A. offered a group of sincere supporters who had all been at rock bottom. They were older people yet they identified with everything I was going through. Had I known these people had my best interest at heart, I would've done things differently.

12 steps are crucially important in our lives.

Lil Jay had a great supporting cast in which he started utilizing before leaving. There were so many people behind him due to his character and talents. He and I used to rap against one another. This was our way of mentally besting the other. He had a very comical side so he would make people laugh at me as he rapped. I could dance so I would have to perform with my raps to win them back over. Big Daddy Kane, Dana Dame, Kool G Rap, Just Ice, Mixx Master Spade, 2 Live Crew were a few of my favorites at that time. O yeah, LL Cool J and Public Enemy must be included along with NWA, Ice T, King T, Dred Scot and Boogie Down Production. I used to be in the dictionary learning words like Big Daddy Kane used in his raps to best Lil Jay. If you know anything about old school hip hop, Lil Jay put you in the mindset of Biz Markie or Digital Underground. We would go at it but in a friendly way.

In No Sense of the word should I have failed after going through Rutherford House but I did because I didn't interject the programming. Actually, In No Sense of the imagination should I have had to go through the Rutherford House because there were good people in society trying to steer me right. I just didn't listen.

During the summer, we all had a job which we were paid as regular civilians. It was during the early part of summer that Lil Jay was released and I took on his role. I can remember him returning to visit as we all worked on tearing down a section

CHAPTER 7

of the school and rebuilding it. Everybody ran to him like he was royalty. I gave them their time because he and I had been talking on the phone so I knew he would be there. Guys from my hood were now in the Rutherford House. When they saw Lil Jay and I embrace, it kind of threw them. Lil Jay and I talked about teaming up when I came home since my release day was getting closer. He told me about the temptations that were coming at him and how he was dealing with them. I advised him to beware of his so-called homies after he told me about some things that had transpired. He said he wasn't hanging with them anymore and that Fonda, an employee at the Rutherford House, was helping him find a job.

Shan, my oldest, was approaching her one year old birthday. Softball season started so we would go practice right by the interstate. I tried out for the pitcher position and got it. I had already played the position during school. Another guy also went for the position. He had his heart set on it and it hurt him when he didn't get it. He seemed to be an okay guy. He played for a rival high school so I felt he could carry his weight. This gave me the incentive to find another position where the team was weaker at. Seeing that right field needed some help, I offered to give the other guy the pitcher position and I played the field. I was eventually the backup pitcher. Our team went undefeated and was given an opportunity to travel to Baton Rouge to participate in a tournament, which we also won. Those were great times.

I learned that one of my childhood friends, Eric Coley, was killed. I heard the news from LaShawnita (TreDavious White of the Buffalo Bills' mother). It crushed me because he had started to get his life back on track. It was revealed that Eric had been a victim of a friend's double cross.

While at the Rutherford House, I was growing mentally and learning a lot. A whole new world opened up to me but I couldn't see it clearly. One night (our bowling night), we were asked to bowl against a professional team due to their opponents not showing up. There I was a kid from the Cooper Road with gold teeth, who gang banged, being asked to bowl against professional bowlers. No one expected me to know how to bowl - a typical case of judging a book by its cover. Growing up, my aunt Pearl often took me to the bowling alley so I already knew how to bowl and keep score. I was matched up against their best player and I beat him to everyone's surprise. I was asked to join their team but unfortunately, I was still locked up. Pam, one of the staffers at the Rutherford House, and I became very close during my stay. She introduced me to her mother.

We were so close in fact that those watching would have thought we were a couple, but of course, we weren't.

Chapter 8

In No Sense does it take sense to commit a crime. Anybody can commit a crime. There is no school for crime, only prison, therefore, it requires no studying; there are no tests; no grade point averages, nothing.

In No Sense does it take sense to abuse drugs and alcohol. Although some of the most intelligent, gifted, and talented people may succumb to using either or both. They were doing so out of senselessness. Both drugs and alcohol harm you more than they do you good, sure the temporary escape helps you to feel good but reality always returns.

Lil Jay was murdered three days after our last embrace. It wasn't a rival Crip gang member that murdered him, it was a friend. His murder devastated the Rutherford House. I learned of him being shot just after it happened. I was asleep when John came to wake me, asking me to come to the office. When I came in and sat down, he told me to pray for Lil Jay because he had been shot. I went back to my room, prayed, and went back to sleep. Approximately an hour later, Pam and Fonda woke me up again. I thought this strange because neither of them worked graveyard shift. Their eyes were swollen and they were holding me tightly, tears soaking through my shirt. I can remember being scared because Pam was touching me inappropriately (by inappropriately, I mean she was hugging me, something that wasn't normal). My cousin, Alvin Jr., was running through my mind, yet I was trying to remain calm knowing Pam was different. They brought me to the office and really cried while holding me. Pam said, "Terrance, I'm not letting you go home to die because I will die if something happened to you." This confused me.

Fonda looked at me as she cried and said, "Lil Jay died...Terrance...Terrance we will do anything for you, so you don't end up like that."

I felt hopeless, helpless, and hurt. By being a member of the blue rag gang (Crips), I had been conditioned to hate the red rag (Bloods) and those representing it but all of that went out the window for Lil Jay. I hadn't been totally robbed of my emotions, so a few tears did fall and I did hurt because I knew he could've done a lot of positive things. Yet his life had been cut short by a friend, a homie.

In No Sense should we destroy innocence.

Lil Jay's death placed me under scrutiny from everyone due to our similar personalities and our leadership. It also placed me on edge but an edge of a different type. By him dying by the hands of his homie, I was on edge of watching for signs of a power struggle due to my personality. Life for me was like this, I had earned a big name that kept getting bigger through talk and this led to my overshadowing some true hood heavyweights. Some took this to heart while others didn't want the fame so they were cool with the "young homie" having the name and fame. It was a very fine line to tow, something I never gave notice to until Lil Jay was killed. Being on edge like that caused a reaction quicker with more force than called for. It bordered on paranoia because it was a known fact that someone was lurking in the shadows to gain fame from your name.

Worrying about how others felt about you or what they had to say about you was very dangerous and deadly. This was peer pressure in which was pure pressure.

There were so many lessons my mom and aunts taught me to keep me from going to jail, so much of which I placed to the side due to falling prey to the pure pressure of what people thought or would think about me. I can remember a time when I was suspended from school. My mom was sick. My aunts came over and they all wanted to beat me just as they had done my dad when I was a kid. Pearl took the diplomatic approach while Baesister (Lettie) and Birdia fumed but eased off. On this day, all of them talked to me about it being a better way to solve problems other than fighting. They told me to learn to talk things out.

In No Sense using the street way is to act before the next man does.

I only had one fight during my time at the Rutherford House. It was after Lil Jay's death. I just stopped caring briefly. We were on break at school and this hip white guy from New Orleans started talking about what he would do if we were in New Orleans. So, I was like, "act like we are there and do it." He was like, "N", you wouldn't…" and before he could finish, I was all over him. Thoughts of being on the cusp of freedom didn't register. I reacted to the negative reference of the "N" word directed towards me. I couldn't see a way to talk it out because when the guy said it, I didn't hesitate or give him a chance to apologize. Luckily we weren't caught.

Conflict in life is a given. We all will go through it; yet it's our handling of it is what matters. How does the majority of the world resolve conflict without it getting bloody and inflating the prison population more? They give themselves time to think, talk out the situation to resolve it, and they compromise. By employing this method, we invoke empathy while thinking around our anger. If we think within our anger and allow it to reach that boiling point, our thinking stops and our reacting starts. We must always give ourselves time to cool off, time to talk to ourselves, time to see where things could lead if we don't reel ourselves back in. Most conflicts, if not resolved, turn out to be much bigger than expected or anticipated.

If a person means you good, they will always talk positive words to you in any situation because there is resolve in everything we get involved with. If your circle of friends is always promoting negativity, choose new friends because you'll be the one who's paying the price while they're free to do as they please. Those who we surround ourselves with are our support system. We must know who has our best interest at heart. Sometimes we get blinded by fake friendship and it costs us dearly. This is why positives are always better than negatives.

Chapter 9

I was released from Rutherford House approximately two and a half months after Lil Jay's and Eric's death. Of the three year sentence, I only served approximately five months. My behavior was so exemplary that staff at Rutherford House spoke to the judge on my behalf and I was released far earlier than expected. I was so elated.

Pam made it her business to stay in touch with me even though she was afraid to visit, fearing someone might mistake her for the police and harm her. Before I left, she cried on my shoulder again and made me promise that I wouldn't end up dead. I made the promise.

With both Eric's and Lil Jay's death fresh on my mind, I didn't return to society with the right attitude. I went against the positive programming that I was exposed to at the Rutherford House and returned to my old ways and my old homies. Most of them had held me down so there wasn't any animosity. While I was locked up, I often thought about positive friends like GG, Roderick Allen, Jeff (CuznJed), Quincie Foster, Quinton Grey, Roovelroe Swan (my youngest daughter's uncle), Lil Willie, Pat and Darryl Drew, and Dartangan (Dot). I knew they would keep me out of trouble because they would always surround themselves with good clean fun and situations. However, I returned to hearing how much money Champ was making, how White Boy was doing his thang, how G was making power moves, how Big Mark and Maine were bringing the Cali boys down to Shreveport, how JoJo Ward was cutting up, how Tinky nem were doing their thang. All of this still excited me, so I fell back in with my trues and resumed living as though I was invincible to being caught. All the lessons I learned about drinking and smoking were forgotten as I got back to picking up the bottle and smoking. I was so busy living until I didn't think of the vicious cycle I once again had joined, a cycle of selfishness and immaturity that totally lacked love and concern for my family, those who I had hurt while I was away.

My attitude was toxic and very "I don't give a damn." Pac would say years later how people loved this attitude yet it's with blindness we're seeing the world when we say this because the majority of the world is fearful of these types of attitudes. People in general actually love caring/positive attitudes. They respond better to a smile as opposed to that frown the hood expects you to display. A friendly greeting of "hi" to a stranger will open friendly doors over the silence of not wanting to appear too friendly. Attitude is everything. It takes you far or for only a short distance. Good attitudes are designed for positivity.

I hadn't set any goals outside of not letting anyone kill me, especially a friend; a meager goal for anyone, yet this was my internal goal. Society hadn't changed to me. I came home practically every weekend so I remained ingrained in the make-up of change.

Upon walking free, I had my act together or at least I thought so but it was far from the truth. I lost focus by losing faith in something that came by way of my living for Satan. I literally cut

CHAPTER 9

off all communication with God and strictly lived to represent the negative elements of my hood.

I had become the dumb version of my cousin, Wolf.

My favorite songs were "My Philosophy" by Boogie Down Productions, "Road to The Riches" by Kool G Rap, "Raw" by Big Daddy Kane, "I got It Made" by Special Ed, and "If It Ain't Rough It Ain't Me" by NWA. But if you want to know the most influential song for me, it was "Gangsta" by NWA. That song really did it for me.

I returned to a war within my head that raged far and wide as soon as I landed. I became the biggest target. Paradoxically, I started reinventing the serenity prayer to where it fit my psyche. I felt as though I was gangsta enough to change things and possessed the smarts to survive within the treachery and conniving. That imagined invincibility of youth rode me.

More and more people around me were being killed. I started drinking more to cope with the pressures of day to day survival of war, even though the drinking forced me to let my guard down more than being sober would.

Those who truly wanted to support me would call my mother to intervene, but I had become unreachable. After being free for a month without honoring one stipulation, I was called back to the Rutherford House and was held with the intention of being shipped to a likewise facility in New Orleans, Louisiana until I turned 18. This crushed me.

Three days later, I escaped. I was 16 years old.

I didn't want to be locked up again especially so far away from home. I thought of the pain I caused for my family, but I felt like a demon possessed because I couldn't stop walking down that path of destruction.

Pam and Fonda continued to show their concern for me. They

feared my steps were increasingly becoming like Lil Jay's but I rationed my steps were my very own.

Then an older yet close homie was killed standing right next to me, shot in the head.

I had returned to the normalcy I knew to be abnormal. I didn't want that existence for my daughters. This was why I did so much to add respect to my name so that they, along with my brother and younger cousins, could walk the streets unharmed and without having to do anything that would jeopardize their freedom.

But, In No Sense was I using sense. I merely reacted or acted without thinking. In No Sense did I sense anything.

Photo Memories

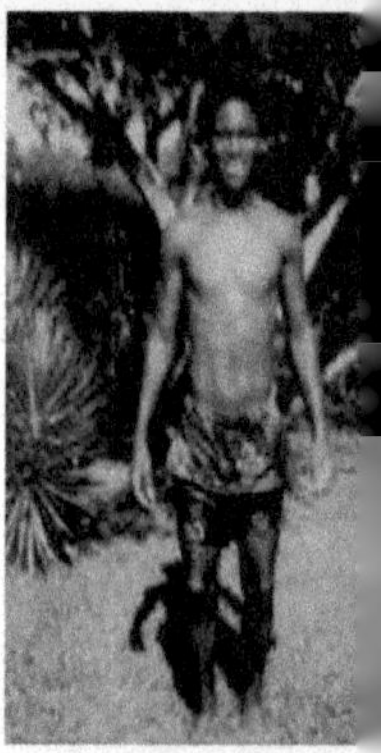

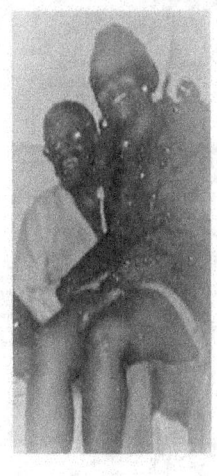

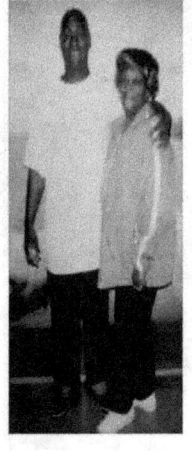
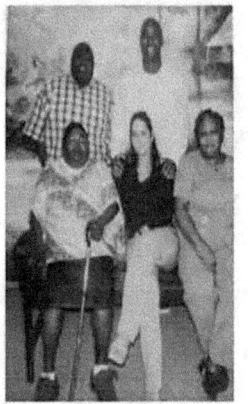

Chapter 10

Just over a month later, I spent Christmas with my youngest daughter and her mother. When they left, I went to the hangout spot where some of my homies were. We started drinking and smoking weed before the idea of going out partying came up. I really didn't want to go. Something was bothering me as it had Lisa (Shaminique's mother) earlier that day. Everyone knew me for being a partier, yet this night I didn't want to go but my homies talked me into going. En route to the party, we drank, smoked, and for the very first time, I snorted cocaine. When we arrived to the party, I was floating. We went inside and partied until the party ended early due to so many fights.

Outside I had a fight and my anger over the fight led to my shooting DeJuan Lewis and killing Jeffrey Owens, an innocent man. This was the worse thing I had ever done in my life.

I was only 16 years old and the juvenile judge decided to try me as an adult. I was taken from juvey hall and placed in the parish jail where there were several hits on my head. The two people who were most likely to succeed had essentially died.

A month before I was set to go to trial, my lawyers came to me with a plea offer while we were inside the courtroom. The deal was that I would receive a 36 year sentence. I quickly refused the offer. My thoughts at the time were I would do more time in prison than I had lived in society. It had also crossed my mind the shorter sentences being given out to others who had committed the same crime. No one was receiving life sentences; no one was receiving anything in the 20 year margin; yet I was offered 36 years. The two whites who instigated the riots didn't even receive 10 years; neither was sentenced beyond 8 years.

Well, when I refused the plea deal, my lawyer and the District Attorney asked the judge for a side bar (this meant they both wen to stand before the judge and spoke low enough as to only hear what the other was saying). After the meeting, the judge addressed me. He told me that he was granting my mother a special visit to speak to me during recess. I was taken back upstairs and placed in the holding tank. Approximately five minutes later, my name was called. I walked the short distance to the attorney's visit room where my mother and LaShonda (my oldest daughter's mother) sat waiting.

This is so hard for me to talk about because this had to be the most ignorant time of my life. There we were alone in that room and my mother begged me to accept the plea deal as opposed to going to trial. I asked my mother to trust my decision not to accept the plea deal. Shonda also tried to convince me to take the plea. She went as far as proposing to me just to give me the assurance/insurance of her not leaving me during my time away. I verbally assaulted her by saying, "Shonda, you're not going to be the one doing that time."

In March 1991, because I did not take the deal, I received a life sentence to be served in the Louisiana State Penitentiary in Angola, Louisiana. I was 17 years old. This was the same prison that my cousins, Alvin Moore Jr, and Irwin Winn, had died.

CHAPTER 10

My mother had essentially lost two sons, both at the age of 16.

Prison is a place of hindsight as opposed to society where foresight is often used. People in the real world of freedom have to keep their eyes up the road more than not, while in prison, you look back over your past and see what led you to doing what you did to get you there. Some guys don't because it is who they are while a lot of guys want better.

Anger had always been my problem. Having a quick temper and acting quickly kept you winning in the street where compromising was hardly an option. The quickest to the draw was usually the winner. We see it everywhere in life so it's not uncommon; yet only in movies do we see the culprit walk away. In prison, early on when I first arrived, violence was the norm. So you could work on your anger in one or two ways; you could continue on the course you were on that brought you to prison or you could work on changing yourself. Again in the early stages there weren't programs for improvement because Angola was still in the shadows of its former self and that was being the bloodiest prison.

Self-reflection and taking responsibility are key components of bettering yourself. Most people that commit crime don't truly understand how far reaching crime is. Initially, I didn't think about my crime because I didn't' want to feel the pain from what I did. I was the youngest guy in Angola so I talked to the guys as they talked to me - through crime. Positive talk didn't get spoken often. That is why I enrolled in school, so that my mind didn't become too corroded with the negative.

There was an old school super smart inmate counselor by the name of Berle, who opened my eyes about a lot of things pertaining to law. After my first fight, he really took an interest in wanting to see me free as well as succeed. Most of the guys there at the time had bad attitudes and didn't care about the next man.

My inability to control my anger led me to prison for life for killing an innocent man. I hid the pain I felt about that because Angola then was dominated by predators, so you couldn't show your human side or you became prey. I had to suppress the pain in order to survive as a 17-year-old incarcerated with adults. There wasn't an atmosphere for repentance or showing remorse. You just had to do what you had to do to not be prey. Berle was an exception. He told me to work on my attitude and not become an angry, bitter young man with no direction or I would die there for catching another murder. He told me to work on my anger and to stop allowing people to get under my skin so easily. It took me a while but I took heed to what he said.

Anger is unavoidable. We all have it yet not everyone allows it to control them nor do most people allow it to reach a boiling point. Most people know how to get around their anger triggers so that the outcome is always peaceful. Some are like I was, using anger to keep them always on edge and on the attack so as not to be the victim. This isn't good because your reaction is always overboard and far too aggressive.

My earlier years at Angola were years of establishing myself and dealing with things as dictated by my new environment. I participated in sports and did things rebelliously as my youth called for. There wasn't much positivity going on.

Coming through the parish jail, you're around people you know from society, both those who are for and those against you. There's still the pure pressure while establishing yourself as being a man who can handle incarcerated life. There was hardly any time for attitude readjustment because the same things you confronted in free society are right there for you to deal with while incarcerated. These occurrences confront adults. Now imagine how a child's mind deals with it, especially when there are those who want the child to not succeed. How must this child rally to win in the negative while fighting to stay sane? It's a very harsh reality of harshness for this developing child that was arrested during development. The child has to do ten times more than an adult that's incarcerated to maintain or develop humanity qualities. It is not easy (especially not during early years where regaining freedom was very hard to accomplish) to place a road of positivity in a child's mind when negativity is the norm.

Chapter 11

During my first seven years and four months in Angola, I had 55 write-ups because I was trying to figure things out and show that I was a man amongst men. I had a rebellious streak and I was learning so much about our history that school didn't teach. This added to my rebelliousness. This made me refuse to pick cotton which was a big thing during that time. I was just gaining an identity.

In No Sense did it make sense to me that I, a sixteen/seventeen year old kid should have been given a life sentence when Tammy Vergos (the woman who shot and killed William McKinney that sparked the Shreveport riot in 1988) and Jason Willis (who shot and killed Darren Martin at the Hot Biscuit) had only received short sentences and we all were in the parish together for the same crimes.

Only one of the guys who served time with me at the Rutherford House came through Angola during my first seven years and four months as opposed to those I knew who went down south to LTI (Louisiana Training Institute). Practically everyone there were there with me in Angola. I also noted that very few guys were there as a first time crime offender. Most guys who were there had committed crimes before so I had previously met some of them along the way. I met people from

CHAPTER 11

other cities or towns who were also sentenced to Angola. In seven years and four months, I was twenty-four years old. The only person I knew from the boy's home had come and gone.

I was coping with murdering Jeffrey Owens the only way available to me – smoking marijuana. There wasn't any talking out my problems. I smoked and read books. I also got my GED within the first six months and started tutoring other guys who wanted to learn.

Reading is the best tool for learning in prison. It opens your mind to a whole other world and gives you a lot of ideas for bettering yourself, family, and community, amongst other things. Through reading and observing, as well as wanting to change myself, I started leaning towards giving up my drug usage. I came to terms with myself and those old AA steps started returning.

My life had become unmanageable from society to prison, leading to me having compulsive behavior. So, I first admitted to myself that I was powerless over my addiction. Initially, I tried to quit on my own because I felt that I had the knowledge and will power to do so, yet God wouldn't be denied the opportunity to show His love. So, I prayed for the strength and will power to never smoke or drink again. As of this day in the summer months of 2020, I have done neither since the Fall of 1995 and I don't feel compelled to indulge in either. My will power remains intact.

I learned to listen and take heed more because the older heads had walked in my shoes so they had to know my struggle. Of course while simultaneously living my own life, I constantly got my feet tangled due to imperfection and standing firmly on principles. I was like a lot of others. I lived my life according to me yet in hindsight, I realized that had I listened, I could have avoided taking Jeffrey's life, shooting DeJuan and serving thirty years, six months in prison. Sometimes listening is the best thing to do.

God is a key factor when we're honestly trying to change. I haven't expounded on God because everyone has their own belief system and I'm not one to say what's right for the next person, however, I will say this, as long as you're true to what you believe and you're trying to live righteously by doing the right thing, you're good in my book.

Allah has been good/great to me.

A lot of my peers (guys I met at the parish jail), childhood friends, banging comrades, etc., started coming to Angola in droves. Homies like Too Short, Anthony Boult, Rob Richardson, Keith Morse, and Leonard Thomas all arrived with growing on their minds. No one wanted to be the same person they were before prison. The end of the road for the living is prison, so you either wake up and become a responsible being or you fail at life and die a nobody.

While in prison, Markey Cannon and I became really close. We formed a brother bond. The reason I mention him is this, he and Lil Jay were cousins.

My eyes were opened a lot during those years. Being sober while working on my anger really humbled me and made me better. I denounced self-hatred and embraced being a man worthy of ushering in positive changes if given another opportunity at freedom.

I lost quite a few supporting homies during that time, yet Half Pint and Donnie Charles' murders affected me the most. Again, a childhood friend had taken Half Pint's life so I faced this dilemma once more.

There were pressures combined with temptation, yet I never

CHAPTER 11

returned to using drugs or alcohol. I prayed a lot, relied on the Creator more, and learned to do a lot of positive self-talking to keep me straight.

Then the homie, Willie Barfield, died in prison as a young man. He was serving a very long sentence for robbery and murder. Drug overdose is the reason for his death.

Many nights I thought before going to sleep, "I wish I had listened." Many nights I regretted my actions on Christmas night because Jeffrey would be alive.

In prison you can hide from reality because you don't see it every day. You're isolated from the rest of the world so there's a lot to take your mind off of what you've done. Prison dulls your memory and robs you of emotion so thoroughly until it's hard for you to see or feel how common people feel.

Chapter 12

The first twenty years of my incarceration were spent in Angola without ever leaving the gates to see free society. I noted my time incarcerated through missed musical eras such as I missed the Death Row era, Sick Wid It, Bad Boy, Tommy Boy, Flava Unit, Flip Mode, Duck Down, No Limit, Ruff Ryder, Rocafella, Cash Money, Slip N Slide, DTP, Tupac, Big Ron, Souljah Slim, Pastor Troy, Poor Righteous Teachers, X Clan, Grand Hustle, Three 6 Mafia, R Kelly, Trey Songz, Aaron Hall, Dave Hollister, NeYo, Anthony Hamilton, Usher, Mariah Carey, So Def, etc.

My first time back in free society while incarcerated was for my mother's funeral. Words cannot capture how I felt or feel. My refusal to listen is the reason I never saw my mother alive again as a free man. This is a harsh reality to live with. My mother loved me through her words and actions, yet I let her down by trying to live life how I saw fit. My mother went to her death bed wanting to see me free. That was love on a level people dream of and it is devastating that she is not here to love me. These falling tears don't stop the pain because it feels like my love for her wasn't comparable to the love she showed to me.

The thing that hurt me most about my mother's death is the

CHAPTER 12

fact of her not seeing me be the son she knew she'd birthed. She died telling her three sisters and son to make sure I came home. I was lost without her and it took me awhile to reach the maturity needed to bring back positives over negatives.

Usher's "Ready to Sign These Papers" and Jay Z's "Blueprint 3" were hot at the time. I will forever remember these two artists and their hits (Jay Z had two singles out, Empire State of Mind and We Gone Run This Town) because of my mother's funeral. I was blessed beyond measure while incarcerated and to Allah all praises are due. Being in Angola, I saw a lot of stand-up guys, both from society onto prison doing time alone, no friends or family support. It was hard to be placed in such a place of hardship without anyone to call on. Yet it happened. Coming from a gang culture in which Shreveport was, your set is supposed to see you through times like that or when you come through regular lifestyles which the game is without gangs, friends are supposed to be there. I'm here to tell you that wasn't reality. Reality was this - you're most likely to do it alone, with only family support, if family is strong enough to stand by you. I'm specifically speaking of friends and homies who stood by me through thirty years of imprisonment. My family never wavered and when my mom died, my aunts each adopted me and continued loving me as though I was their own. My cousins continued loving me, some of who were born while I was in prison. Champ, G (and the whole Young family), GG, KoKo, White Boy, Cuzn Jed, Iron Mike D, Wacca, etc, all held me down and vicariously through them some of the younger generations know who I am. I'm not lost on the legacy of the Cooper Road.

In No Sense should it take prison to teach you how to be a good responsible human being. If you wait to reach this stage to start using the tools you first learned at home then through others along the way, you've waited too long. In most cases, second chances aren't offered, therefore, we must make the first chance count. We simply must give ourselves time to think; just a little time will save us a world of grief.

Patience is learned while serving time. Once you learn the importance of patience you learn self-control. We need self-control to make us better humans. It's an internal thing. We simply have to be in tune to. Most people use it. This is why the overwhelming majority hasn't let go and go on rampages. People prioritize self-control and emphasize empathy; therefore, they don't become unglued over the slightest disagreement.

It took a lot of patience for 2012 to get here and change my life from Atkins v VA (in 2002 the U.S. Supreme Court ruled it unconstitutional to kill a mentally challenged person), onto Roper (in 2005, the U. S. Supreme Court used its ruling in Atkins to determine that a kid's brain was just as underdeveloped as someone mentally challenged so it was ruled unconstitutional to kill a child seventeen years old and under). Then in 2010, the Graham ruling by the U.S. Supreme Court said that a child seventeen years old and under who hadn't committed a homicide couldn't receive a life sentence. On to Miller in 2012, the U.S. Supreme court ruled it unconstitutional to give a child seventeen years old and under who had committed a homicide, mandatory life sentences. This ruling was met by resistance in some states, namely Louisiana, which accepted the high court's ruling yet said it didn't apply retroactively. It took four more years (Montgomery) before the U.S. Supreme Court would hear the case again and rule it to be retroactive, meaning all those who had been sentenced before 2012 could benefit from the law change.

CHAPTER 12

Montgomery gave me the hope I had prayed for throughout the twenty-six years I had been imprisoned. I could finally smell freedom, yet I hadn't reached the maturity Allah demanded of me so I kept getting senseless write-ups which kept me imprisoned longer.

The year of Montgomery's ruling, I lost my OG homie, Cebren "CBo" Stokes, in prison. This had an effect on me in a positive manner because he had been a model for change. He had also been the person who put together Montgomery's case, living long enough to see the work he'd so selflessly done take center stage country wide. From childhood he had taught me a lot. I was arrested at his sister's crib in the projects. RIP C-BO!

From the death of my mother, I formed a new addiction, one I justified as not being harmful to self or others. That addiction was with cellphones. After being confined so long without being in touch with society, that little small device offered me a glimpse of how freedom looked and I couldn't turn away. That addiction, however accepted in society, was against prison rules so for the next few years, I would get busted with them, receive reports, costing me more years confined.

Chapter 13

The majority of my time in Angola was spent behind structural thinking of not only a convict but also that of an outlaw, meaning nothing was to ever be taken to security. Whatever happened, you handled it. That also meant that you didn't form allegiances with security because unlike most prisons in America, prisoners and security worked close around as well as with one another. However, January 19, 2018, I changed my thinking when I authored a letter with Frederick "Boobie Earl" Thompson in which included eleven other juvenile lifers (Willie Platter, Jameel Malik, Terrance Simon, Dwight Carter, Melvin Mingo, Antonio Jackson, Clifford Green, Herman Trudeau, Henry Montgomery, Troy Young, and Barry Pasoul) to meet with Warden Vannoy asking him for help so that we could have a better chance at making parole. At this meeting with Warden Vannoy, was every warden at the prison. We spoke and reached a good understanding. The meeting was the first of its kind and it had an impact.

After the meeting, Assistant Warden Anne Marie Easley saw something special in us as a group and decided she would start Victim Awareness with us. This kicked off a string of positive changes throughout the prison.

CHAPTER 13

Here's a breakdown of this group. We all knew one another for over twenty years and we were all stand up guys. With all of our years of knowing each other, Victim Awareness taught us just how little we knew intimate details of the other. In prison, few people ask the other about their crime. It's just not something people did. Yet in Victim Awareness, you're stripped of the armor and you must bare your soul. Through this group, we showed our vulnerability and we became real friends and family.

At no time during my incarceration had I ever had security have my back. Keep in mind my introduction into prison came during the rough years, so I lived on the opposite side of their rules but through the family of Victim Awareness, that changed. Warden Easley became our sister of sorts. She had our backs and we had hers. This made us more receptive of learning the intricacies of our crime.

For the first time most of us were confronting our crimes face to face in a group setting and more times than not, with the tough guy stripped away. The pain spilled over and collectively, as a family, we cried, accepted responsibility for taking life and subsequently negatively impacting the lives of family members and friends (secondary victims), community (tertiary victims) and as in my crime DeJuan Lewis and Jeffrey Owens (primary victims). Thoughts surrounding our crimes and those who were impacted hadn't been thought of until we took Victim Awareness.

The far reach of crime was lost on me until taking that class. I never really understood how property lost its value in high crime areas nor how people watching crime on the news fell into the category of tertiary victims. Learning the effects of victimization, grief and so on effectively changed me forever.

Through Victim Awareness, we all appeared on Dateline with Lester Holt, another positive and wonderful experience.

We got a chance to attend a victim conference where we listened to actual victims speak and we met them. That was also a life-changing event.

I matured through that because I accepted responsibility and I didn't want to be the bad apple. The prison viewed me as the likeliest to mess up due to my vice being known by practically everyone. There was a mark on my head because of my past failures that brought about all the write-ups (at this point I had 140). But I refused to be the person to tarnish the image of our family. Plus, they were my support group helping me fight my addiction. Each time I felt myself about to get another phone, I leaned on them.

Herman Tureaud made parole early on and we celebrated his freedom.

Willie Platter went before the board right before the group formed and to our surprise, his parole was not granted. The surprise came due to how well his conduct was and how he had changed.

Troy Young appeared a couple of months after Herman. Again, surprise came when he was also denied parole.

After Troy, Henry Montgomery (the man whose case was used to place us in the position of a second chance) went before the board and was denied. His denial was felt far and wide because we were appearing on Dateline at the time of his hearing so the world was allowed a chance to see it and feel some of our pain.

Dwight got transferred to another prison.

At the time of Montgomery's hearing, there was a beautiful set-up where former prisoners could return and show support. Montgomery had lots of supporters as did our other comrades

CHAPTER 13

because guys actually came to see other's walk free. Plus we were kids at the time our offenses. This stuck with people also.

My turn came and I was granted parole, surprising quite a lot of people.

Antonio will have gone before the board before this is published as well as Boobie Earl (initially he was scheduled to go on the same board as I). I will be on Zoom showing my brothers support.

Clifford will also go up again (his first hearing was before Victim Awareness started) this year.

Chapter 14

There are a lot of gaps in thirty years because for the most part it was a redundant routine of boredom. Every day was practically the same. You woke up at 5 am when the lights came on, took care of your hygiene and got ready for breakfast, returned from the chow hall, used the restroom, and then you await for work call to be called loudly with a whistle. If you were a field worker, there was the regular rhetoric of slavery. If your job was elsewhere, you just went. For those who go visit, you looked forward to the weekend. Everybody was ready for 3 pm because the workday was over. Some went to the law library after work call was over. Others went to church or other calls out until 10 pm and returned to the dorm to go to sleep and get ready for the next day.

Just as some friendships can't withstand the separation, most relationships die either before the judge says "life" or not long after. I went to jail in a relationship, yet I came to prison one year and six months later single. I never expected anything more because not every girl is made of the same stuff as Coretta Scott King, Winnie Mandela, or my homie Mrs. Fox Rich. It takes a very special human to stay beside you while going through prison, a very special woman to take up your cause and fight for your freedom. Along my journey, I had the pleasure of

CHAPTER 14

enjoying the momentary commitment of some extraordinary women but time away causes the body to stray even when the mind wants to stay. Doing time is hard on a prisoner, therefore, it's double hard on the person on the outside whose doing it with you.

Fox Rich is a special case in my estimation so I will highlight this beautiful woman. My homie, Rob Richardson, is her husband. Rob was recently released after doing twenty-two years and she held him down throughout. Twice a month visits (which extended during the good times of Angola when banquets were frequently held), his account kept money, his kids knew their dad, and she fought to get him free until he was freed.

Cammie Maturin is another standout woman to me. Unlike Fox Rich, who was married to Rob before prison, Cami met her husband when she came to the prison with a tour. The meeting led to address exchange, letter writing, phone calls, visits, and marriage. Her husband, Sirvoris Sutton, and I are good friends. He's an Atlanta native. Cami is a front line soldier elite. She has become one of the most recognizable faces for prison reform in Louisiana.

I highlight these women because I know their dedication to their husbands and their love is binding. Years and years, I prayed for a woman of their cloth but women of this ilk are rarities. You don't just run across them in prison. This type of woman is that rare gem you must know how to love and cherish once you have her.

A few more standout women, Deilra "Dee" Isaac (Milton "Poppa" Isaac's wife), Alisia Brooks (Adonis "Black" Brook's wife), Shelia Chea (David Chea's wife), Sahron "Punkin" Ellison (Glen "Wubbie" Styles' girl), Vanessa Parkman (Terrance Lair's girl), Dimitri Young (Tyrone "Top" Young's wife). All of these women are true fighters who have gone that extra mile for their men so I applaud them.

By the stretch of the imagination does easy come to mind when thinking of a relationship with someone incarcerated. There are all types of hardships you'll go through and frankly speaking some people are just not geared to be a prisoner's mate. Some prefer remaining single over giving their all to a prisoner. It is what it is.

Love and its beauty are alluring, yet it is elusive to those doing time.

We lost three juvenile lifers along the way. My homie, LaMarcus Morris (who was engaged), Eldridge "Lucious" Dukes (was married) and Wilbert "Nip" Dorsey.

In No Sense should it take incident upon incident to convince you of the consequences being costly.

I lost White Boy, Wacca, Jon (KoKo's brother), Shamell, and Lavelle along the way.

In a way, I think of my past failed relationships the same way as I do my past failures. I have said that I've had some pretty incredible women to pass through my life and I shoulder the blame for them not staying. A lack of maturity on my part is why I think they left. Yes, I feel there were men lurking in the shadows, however, I think I didn't give enough of me in the areas they needed me to. This is why I don't' have anything bad to say about any of them. I cherish the time I was given with them.

I did a lot of letter writing over the years. Before the technological advancement, letters were the route to intimate communication. Judy and I met through letters and we were engaged before things went sour.

Photo Memories

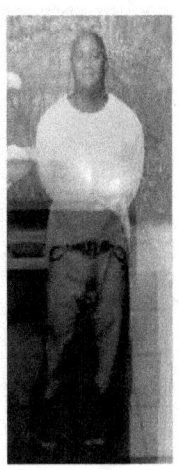

Chapter 15

4 Da Struggle Publishing started as Da Struggle Records in 1998. In 2000, a good friend of mine, Lee Lucas (yes, the same one Kevin Gates raps about), told me to get more creative with the name so we stayed up all night one night at the infamous Camp J and added the 4. I thought of the logo while looking at the image of man's evolution from apes. The history of blacks in America is harsh, a fact no one can overlook since the entrance in 1619 until the abolishment in 1865. After the cruelty was supposed to end, a newer version of the same continued under the legality of imprisonment, thus the logo. Born with one strike, raised with another strike, predicated off the same, you continue growing mentally, maturing so that as an adult you break the chains of oppression.

Not being opposed to the struggle for human decency is the compassion needed for us to continue pushing forward. Being 4 Da Struggle means you're in favor of the next person succeeding or having a second chance for a past mistake. Being 4 Da Struggle means you won't stand by and be a voluntary or involuntary participant in the carefully orchestrated program to annihilate an entire race of people. Being 4 Da Struggle means that you acknowledge the next person respectively and you are willing to assist if assistance is needed.

4 Da Struggle also embodies the African colors of red, black, green, and yellow, the origin of the people of hue.

In No Sense did I allow myself not to know that intelligence is a need to succeed. I learned through studying and I became a better human being to my fellow prisoners. Through my will to want to be better, I started doing better and one day my homie, Boo, challenged me to write a book. I had never done it before so I accepted the challenge and before I knew it, I had written a 400 page novel that I named STREET EDUCATED. I took the name from a collection of poetry I had written. I titled it this due to my tackling intellectual topics without having a college education. I am a man from the streets, equipped with a GED and culinary trade so the combination of STREET went with the Educated. There is no negative connotation associated with the name. In no way am I glorifying street living. In fact, I'm promoting the opposite. Educated shouldn't be taken lightly just because it's next to street. Being educated in any sense is to be learned, to know how to solve things, in the most intelligent manner. In STREET EDUCATED, people are needed so that all of the problems can receive attention and work can start being done to fix the problems. Educated people can bring in the reasons necessary to end the poverty which is a leading reason for crime. Street people become street people when they no longer see school as being a viable resource for making life better. Through the brand of STREET EDUCATED, I plan on changing this philosophy because being educated is the coolest thing. Through the brand of STREET EDUCATED, I plan on teaching the culture important historical dates that changed life for the better.

STREET EDUCATED is fashion promoting the need for education.

CHAPTER 15

For the past twelve years, I have been writing novels, poetry, raps while designing STREET EDUCATED clothing and selling it through the prison. Had the guards not lost my property, I would have forty books completed. My time wasn't idle. STREET EDUCATED has sparked a many intelligent debates on the subject of history.

How do you get to every institution of learning? I hope you said by a street. The street is essential if you want to be educated.

Here's an important fact: If you're not from the street, those who are won't be receptive of you, only a street person will listen to a street person.

You can take a STREET EDUCATED person and place him in any project in America and he/she will win them over because of the authenticity and ability to speak the language of struggle. Now take a Harvard educated person and place him in any project in America and tell me if he will be able to win the people over? A STREET EDUCATED person can bridge the gap between the boardroom and inner city. No one else has the ability to do so because the inner city only opens up to those they identify with. This is why the brand STREET EDUCATED characters dress to resemble the inner city, yet the strength of each character is the books, tassels, diploma, fire hydrant, and the reflection in their glasses of the city. This says education is of extreme importance to change the conditions of those overlooked until tragedy strikes.

I used my thirty years away to educate myself, to become a better human, to learn the value of wanting for fellow man that in which I want for self. I think now because to do so positively will generate the change needed to better things for all. Change has to start somewhere. I say, why not start at the bottom.

I will not support negatives, so please don't think solely

of negatives when thinking of the streets because positives have come from there.

4 Da Struggle is a branch from the tree of human acceptance. It started in the voice of those who sang the songs of love, peace, joy, pain, unity, and justice. 4 Da Struggle is the face of social justice and penal reform – a face for change, a change needed in the country rated as the best in the world. We cannot truly be this greatness if we continue separating people.

Merchandise

1619: Blacks arrived in America in balls and chains, against their will. They were forced into the New World, with new rules and segregation based on skin color.

1865: Freedom under the 13th Amendment came with a price. Jim Crow Laws were created, denying rights and allowing the continuation of slavery through incarceration.

Present Day: From birth life has not been easy because we live in the shadows of a society that treats us differently. Fortunately with growth comes the knowledge that will BREAK THE CHAINS OF OPPRESSION and become a positive force 4 da struggle.

Chapter 16

In No Sense can I truly make sense of my doing thirty years for an avoidable crime if only I would have used my brain to think.

After 30 years 6 months, I walked out of the gates of Angola alongside Assistant Warden Ann Marie Easley into the waiting arms of my cousin, Sha; her mother, Shelia; my aunt/mom, Lettie; aunt Birdia; brother, Moon; cousins, Royelle, Tawanna, LeCarlos; and family friend, Joanna. I felt alive for the first time in 40 years. This was my resurrection of sorts. Immediately after showing love to my family through hugs, I put on the shirt I was supposed to have worn coming through the gates, a RIP Rufus shirt, because this was my brotha from another mother. He had served 18 years alongside me. The streets had tricked my brotha out of his life as it has done so many of us. I wear his face honorably yet as a reminder to never return to the streets.

The world changed on me as I sat on a plantation that was named in mockery of black people from Africa. I was excited about the growth and wanted very much to be a part of it so I just kept mentally preparing myself.

I'm a grandfather of three, Reagan, Jace and Ms. Rah.

Beyond the glitz of my return to society, beyond the happiness and smiles, I also experience some sadness. Of course, I feel constant pain in regards to my mother. That hurt has never left me. I never stop missing her and my tears never dry up. A few days after I walked free from prison, I had a conversation with my brother, Moon. He told me that my mother was badly crushed by my decision not to take the plea deal I was offered. He said she refused to leave home for days and all she did was cry. I can't express the hurt and sadness I feel for the pain I caused my mother but I know in my heart that she never stopped loving me. There is another deep pain that most convicts don't talk about. It's a pain that even I wasn't prepared for. This pain has blindsided me and that is the rejection of your child due to spending so much time apart. As of today, I have been free almost two months and I have yet to see my kids, Shan (my oldest, who has been my biggest gift) and Nique (my youngest). I was never a deadbeat dad but I have been treated as though I was/am. Although this situation is disturbing to me, I can understand that being apart from your dad for 30 years is a lot for a child to handle.

In No Sense could I have envisioned myself enslaved doing the exact same things slaves did a century before me. There was no sense in me ever thinking this possible, yet I did thirty years, 25 a slave.

There are many guys in prison hoping I return. To them, I say thank you for keeping me focused and positive. There is no darkness in my walk. What I do is done in the light. I want to make the world a better place just as I wanted to make prison a better place. My support system is unbelievable. My cousin, Marcellous, had a Porsche awaiting me upon my arrival home and my aunt Lettie gifted me a Beamer. I have built three companies from the bottom up so I am grounded and humbled. I have no reason nor desire to return back to prison. I'M FREE!

Photo Memories

www.ingramcontent.com/pod-product-compliance
Lightning Source LLC
Chambersburg PA
CBHW050506120526
44589CB00046B/1601